What's the Issue?

WHAT ARE VACCINES?

By Simon Pierce

Published in 2023 by
KidHaven Publishing, an Imprint of Greenhaven Publishing, LLC
29 East 21st Street
New York, NY 10010

Designer: Andrea Davison-Bartolotta
Editor: Jennifer Lombardo

Photo credits: Cover (top) sutlafk/Shutterstock.com; cover (bottom) Marlon Lopez MMG1 Design/Shutterstock.com; p. 5 MT PhotoLife/Shutterstock.com; pp. 7, 9 Everett Collection/Shutterstock.com; p. 11 fotohay/Shutterstock.com; p. 13 Zonicboom/Shutterstock.com; p. 15 Ron Adar/Shutterstock.com; p. 17 Baris Acarli/Shutterstock.com; p. 19 Color Symphony/Shutterstock.com; p. 21 Lidiia/Shutterstock.com.

Library of Congress Cataloging-in-Publication Data

Names: Pierce, Simon, author.
Title: What are vaccines? / Simon Pierce.
Description: New York, NY : KidHaven Publishing, [2023] | Series: What's the issue? | Includes index.
Identifiers: LCCN 2022011627 | ISBN 9781534542150 (library binding) | ISBN 9781534542136 (paperback) | ISBN 9781534542143 (set) | ISBN 9781534542167 (ebook)
Subjects: LCSH: Vaccines–Juvenile literature. | Vaccines–History–Juvenile literature. | Vaccination–Juvenile literature.
Classification: LCC RM281 .P54 2023 | DDC 615.3/72–dc23/eng/20220315
LC record available at https://lccn.loc.gov/2022011627

Printed in the United States of America

Some of the images in this book illustrate individuals who are models. The depictions do not imply actual situations or events.

CPSIA compliance information: Batch #CSKH23: For further information contact Greenhaven Publishing LLC, New York, New York at 1-844-317-7404.

Please visit our website, www.greenhavenpublishing.com. For a free color catalog of all our high-quality books, call toll free 1-844-317-7404 or fax 1-844-317-7405.

Find us on

CONTENTS

A Scary Time   4

An Important Year   6

More Vaccines   8

Diseases Coming Back   10

Fear of Vaccines   12

Are Vaccines Safe?   14

What's in Vaccines?   16

Do Vaccines Work?   18

Stopping the Spread   20

Glossary   22

For More Information   23

Index   24

A Scary Time

For much of human history, catching a disease, or sickness, was one of the scariest things that could happen. There are many diseases that can kill people or cause other problems such as **paralysis** or loss of hearing. There was once nothing that could be done to prevent, or stop, someone from catching harmful and sometimes deadly diseases such as measles, whooping cough, scarlet fever, or smallpox.

What changed? It was the **development** of vaccines. These medicines stop most people from getting certain diseases by helping their body recognize and beat the germs that cause those diseases. This is called an immune response.

Facing the Facts

Some parts of the world have fewer vaccinated people. In some cases, this is because vaccines cost more than people can afford. In others, it's because no good vaccine has been developed yet.

Chicken pox used to be a common childhood illness. After scientists developed a vaccine in 1995, the number of cases of chicken pox in the United States fell by 90 percent.

An Important Year

Smallpox was a disease that caused people to develop a fever as well as **blisters** on their skin. There was no medicine for the disease, so it caused millions of deaths around the world. People who didn't die sometimes went blind.

Doctor Edward Jenner wanted to keep people safe from smallpox by stopping them from getting it in the first place. He noticed that people who caught cowpox, which was a much less **severe** disease, didn't get smallpox. In 1796, Jenner put matter from a cowpox blister into scratches on a boy's body. Later, he exposed the boy to smallpox. The boy didn't get sick because the cowpox gave him an immune response to the smallpox.

Facing the Facts

If a disease is gone for good in the world, doctors say it's been eradicated. If it's gone for more than 12 months in one place, they say it's eliminated there. As of 2022, only smallpox has been eradicated.

This picture shows people in New York City lining up for their smallpox vaccine in 1872.

More Vaccines

People used Jenner's idea to make vaccines for more diseases over the years. In the late 1800s, a disease called polio started appearing in the United States, especially in the summers. It was very contagious, or easily spread. Many people who caught polio got better, but thousands were paralyzed. Every summer, communities closed swimming pools and movie theaters to stop polio from spreading.

In 1955, Jonas Salk announced that he had developed a vaccine for polio. People lined up to get it. One of the most feared diseases of the 20th century wasn't a **threat** anymore! By 1994, polio was eliminated in North and South America.

Facing the Facts 🔍

Polio might be eradicated soon. As of 2022, Afghanistan and Pakistan are the only two countries left where polio is endemic, or constantly present.

Some people with polio had to be put into a machine called an iron lung to help them breathe.

Diseases Coming Back

Once certain diseases weren't a threat anymore, people started to forget how bad they could be. Some people started to spread false stories that vaccines were more dangerous, or unsafe, than the diseases. People began to believe this, and some stopped vaccinating their children.

If someone catches a disease while traveling and brings it back to a place where it was once eliminated, they can spread it to unvaccinated people. Measles is a disease that causes tiredness, fever, sneezing, and a red rash all over the body. In 2000, it was declared eliminated in the United States. However, in 2008, unvaccinated kids started catching it again. If any outbreak lasts for a year or more, measles won't be considered eliminated in the United States anymore.

Measles can cause a lot of serious problems. These include **infection** of the eyes, ears, lungs, or liver; brain **damage**; and in some cases, death.

Facing the Facts

Most people only get chicken pox once. Some parents throw chicken pox parties because they think catching the disease will keep their children safer than the vaccine can. However, these parties are dangerous; people can go deaf or die because of chicken pox.

Fear of Vaccines

Since about 1796, there have been anti-vaxxers, or people who believe vaccines are dangerous and don't support their use. This is often because they don't understand how vaccines really work. Some people get scared when they see the lists of **chemicals** that are used to make vaccines.

Other people worry about vaccines' **side effects**. When someone gets vaccinated, their body sometimes reacts as if they'd actually gotten sick. Some people think this means vaccines make people sick. However, it's just what happens when the body learns how to make the **antibodies** that fight a disease.

Facing the Facts 🔍

A small number of people are allergic to some vaccines. This means their body reacts very badly to something that's normally harmless in the vaccine. An allergic reaction generally happens within 30 minutes after someone gets the vaccine.

COMMON SIDE EFFECTS

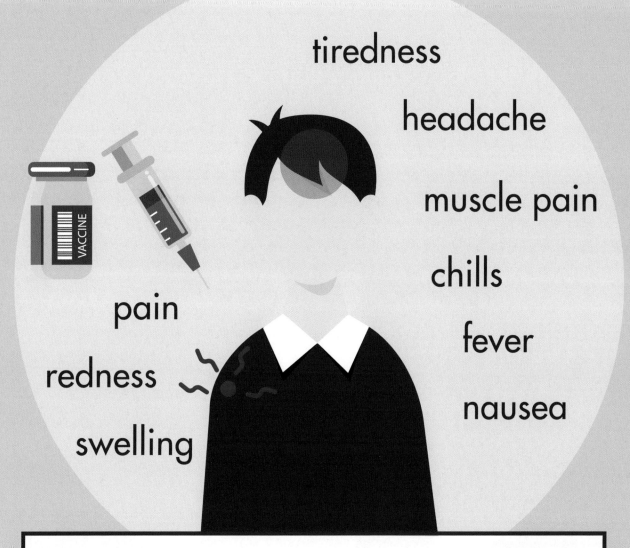

tiredness

headache

muscle pain

chills

fever

nausea

pain

redness

swelling

This picture shows common side effects from the COVID-19 vaccine. These generally go away within 24 hours, unlike the disease, which can last for weeks.

Are Vaccines Safe?

Some people who don't trust vaccines think it's safer to get antibodies by actually catching a disease. However, diseases are unpredictable—they don't act the same way all the time. One person might get measles and be totally fine, while another might go blind.

Vaccines are more predictable, and the side effects are much less severe. Many people have no side effects at all. The vaccine helps the body make antibodies, which fight the disease in the future. The chemicals in vaccines aren't dangerous, and they leave the body in a day or two.

Facing the Facts 🔍

The most common side effect of a vaccine is pain and swelling at the spot where the vaccine was **injected**. Severe side effects aren't common, but they can be similar to the side effects of the disease. For example, people are more likely to get dangerous blood clots from COVID-19 than from the COVID-19 vaccine.

Science has shown that natural immunity, which happens after someone catches a disease, isn't as predictable or long-lasting as vaccine immunity.

What's in Vaccines?

The chemicals in vaccines scare some people. These chemicals often have long names, and it isn't always clear to people exactly what they do. However, things are only put into vaccines if they're both needed and safe. The main ingredient, or part, in most vaccines is a small, weak amount of the virus or bacterium that causes the disease.

Ingredients in vaccines can be found in nature. For example, many vaccines include salts. These help the vaccine work better in the body. Sugar is an ingredient that helps keep the vaccine from going bad while it's being stored.

Facing the Facts

A chemical called formaldehyde is used to keep some vaccines fresh while they're being made. There's almost no formaldehyde in a finished vaccine. In fact, there's more formaldehyde naturally in our bodies than there is in vaccines.

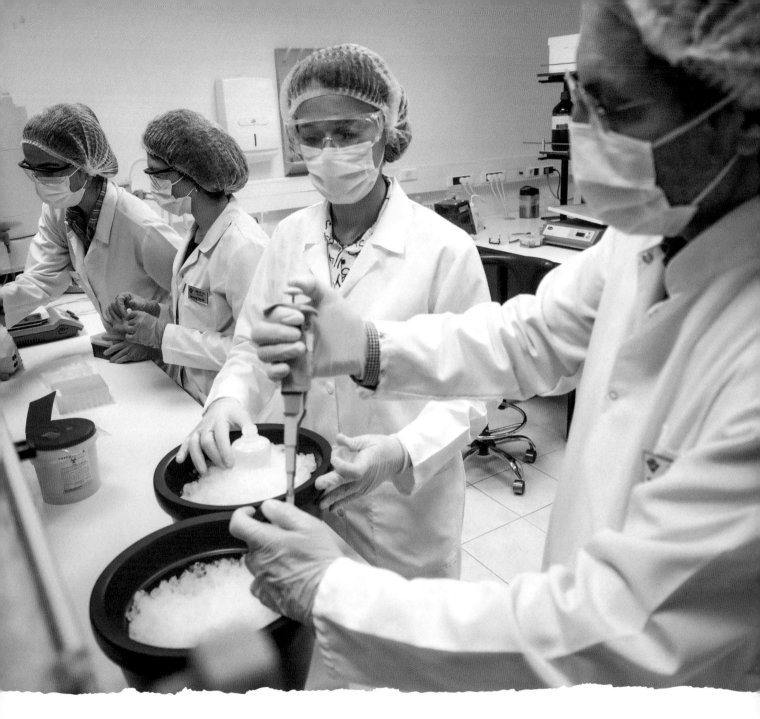

When people learn how science works, it often doesn't seem scary anymore.

Do Vaccines Work?

Some people think there's no point in getting vaccinated because you can sometimes still catch and spread the disease. There's a little bit of truth to this. It's impossible to make a vaccine that's 100 percent **effective**. That's exactly why it's important for everyone to get vaccinated!

The more people are vaccinated, the harder it is for a disease to spread. If someone who's effectively vaccinated catches it, their body often kills the germs before they can spread to other people. When a lot of people in a community are vaccinated, they have **herd immunity**. This keeps people who can't get vaccinated, such as babies or people with a vaccine allergy, safe.

Facing the Facts

Antibodies don't last forever, whether someone gets them from a vaccine or from catching the disease. This is why people often need an extra dose, called a booster shot, for their vaccines.

18

FACT OR FAKE?

Fake	Fact
Vaccine side effects are more dangerous than the disease.	Vaccine side effects are almost always milder than the disease's effects.
Vaccines don't work.	Many diseases have been eliminated or eradicated because of vaccines.
Vaccine ingredients are harmful.	Every vaccine ingredient can be found in nature and is present in very small amounts in a vaccine.
Natural immunity is better.	A vaccine gives you immunity from a disease without the threat of dying or having lifelong problems.
Other people will get vaccinated, so herd immunity will keep me safe.	Herd immunity only works if everyone who can get vaccinated does so.

A lot of untrue things are said about vaccines. Knowing the truth helps keep us all safe.

Stopping the Spread

There's a lot of fake news out there about vaccines. Some anti-vaxxers lie or only tell part of the truth to make it look like they're right. However, others are sure that what they believe is the truth. They just want to do what's best for themselves and their children, and they've been told vaccines are bad.

Misinformation, which is a kind of false statement, spreads very quickly on social media. Some people tend to believe everything they see on the internet. When you see something about vaccines, check it out for yourself before you share it! You can be someone who stops misinformation from spreading—like a vaccine!

Facing the Facts

Some anti-vaxxers think eating healthy foods and exercising regularly will keep them healthy better than vaccines can. However, even the healthiest people can catch a disease and spread it to others.

WHAT CAN YOU DO?

Learn more about the science behind vaccines.

Speak up when you see or hear misinformation.

Get vaccinated.

If you know anti-vaxxers, talk to them about their reasons for not trusting vaccines.

Give people facts to help them fight their fear.

Check what you see online before you share it.

When people trust vaccines, everyone is safer. That's why it's important for everyone to do their part to stop both misinformation and disease from spreading.

GLOSSARY

antibody: A substance produced by the body to fight disease.

blister: A small, raised area of the skin filled with a watery liquid.

chemical: Matter that can be mixed with other matter to cause changes.

damage: Harm done to a person.

development: The act of building, changing, or creating over time.

effective: Producing a wanted result.

herd immunity: A lowered chance of spreading infection within a community that occurs when a certain percentage of the community is immune to the disease.

infection: A sickness caused by germs entering the body.

inject: To force something into the body using a needle or other sharp item.

paralysis: An inability to move.

severe: Hard to bear or deal with.

side effect: An unwanted effect of a drug or chemical that occurs alongside the desired effect.

threat: Something that is likely to cause harm.

FOR MORE INFORMATION

WEBSITES

BrainPop: Vaccines

www.brainpop.com/health/diseasesinjuriesandconditions/vaccines
Learn more about vaccines with Tim and Moby.

Vax Pack Hero

vaxpackhero.com
Defeat germs with the help of vaccine creators in this free game.

BOOKS

Allen, John. *Vaccine Wars: When Science and Politics Collide.* San Diego, CA: ReferencePoint Press, 2022.

Blohm, Craig E. *The Search for a COVID-19 Vaccine.* San Diego, CA: ReferencePoint Press, 2021.

Kaiser, Brianna. *Smallpox: A Vaccine Success.* Minneapolis, MN: Lerner Publications, 2022.

INDEX

A
Afghanistan, 8
antibodies, 12, 14, 18
anti-vaxxers, 12, 20, 21

B
booster shot, 18

C
chemicals, 12, 14, 16
chicken pox, 5, 11
COVID-19, 13, 14
cowpox, 6

G
germs, 4, 18

H
herd immunity, 18, 19

I
immune response, 4, 6

J
Jenner, Edward, 6, 8

M
measles, 4, 10, 11, 14
medicine, 4, 6

P
Pakistan, 8
paralysis, 4, 8
polio, 8, 9

S
Salk, Jonas, 8
scarlet fever, 4
side effects, 12, 13, 14, 19
smallpox, 4, 6, 7

U
United States, 5, 8, 10

W
whooping cough, 4